GAME DAY

GET READY FOR A BASEBALL GAME

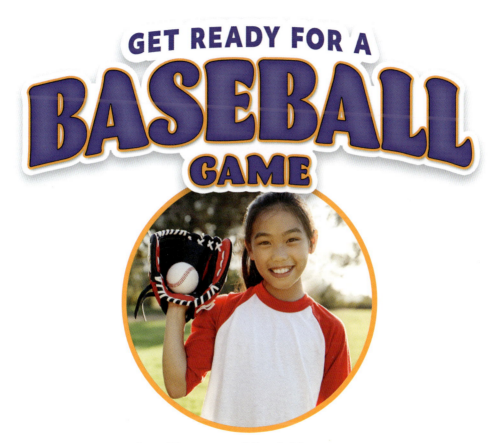

by Emma Huddleston

Consultant: Beth Gambro
Reading Specialist, Yorkville, Illinois

BEARPORT
PUBLISHING

Minneapolis, Minnesota

Teaching Tips

Before Reading

- Look at the cover of the book. Discuss the picture and the title.
- Ask readers to brainstorm a list of what they already know about baseball games. What can they expect to see in this book?
- Go on a picture walk, looking through the pictures to discuss vocabulary and make predictions about the text.

During Reading

- Read for purpose. Encourage readers to think about preparing for a baseball game as they are reading.
- Ask readers to look for the details of the book. What needs to happen before the big game?
- If readers encounter an unknown word, ask them to look at the sounds in the word. Then, ask them to look at the rest of the page. Are there any clues to help them understand?

After Reading

- Encourage readers to pick a buddy and reread the book together.
- Ask readers to name two things from the book that a player does to get ready for a baseball game. Find the pages that tell about these things.
- Ask readers to write or draw something they learned about baseball.

Credits:
Cover and title page, © monkeybusinessimages/iStock; 3,© TerryJ/iStock; 5, © stu99/iStock; 6–7, © SeventyFour/iStock; 8–9, © shapecharge/iStock; 11, © digitalskillet/iStock; 13,© Pgiam/iStock; 15, © RichVintage/iStock; 16–17, © RBFried/iStock; 18–19, © AirImages/Shutterstock; 21, © Hero Images/iStock; 22T, © pics721/Adobe Stock; 22M, © gurineb/iStock; 22B, © jondpatton/iStock; 23TL, © digitalhallway/iStock; 23TM, © DarioGaona/iStock; 23TR, © LeoPatrizi/iStock; 23BL, © P_Wei/iStock; 23BM, © LSOphoto/iStock; and 23BR,© DarioGaona/iStock.

Library of Congress Cataloging-in-Publication Data

Names: Huddleston, Emma, author.
Title: Get ready for a baseball game / by Emma Huddleston.
Description: Minneapolis, Minnesota : Bearport Publishing Company, [2024] |
  Series: Game day | Includes bibliographical references and index.
Identifiers: LCCN 2023002696 (print) | LCCN 2023002697 (ebook) | ISBN
  9798888220597 (library binding) | ISBN 9798888222553 (paperback) | ISBN
  9798888223741 (ebook)
Subjects: LCSH: Baseball--Juvenile literature. | Baseball players--Juvenile
  literature.
Classification: LCC GV867.5 .H83 2024 (print) | LCC GV867.5 (ebook) | DDC
  796.357--dc23/eng/20230126
LC record available at https://lccn.loc.gov/2023002696
LC ebook record available at https://lccn.loc.gov/2023002697

Copyright © 2024 Bearport Publishing Company. All rights reserved. No part of this publication may be reproduced in whole or in part, stored in any retrieval system, or transmitted in any form or by any means, electronic, mechanical, photocopying, recording, or otherwise, without written permission from the publisher.

For more information, write to Bearport Publishing, 5357 Penn Avenue South, Minneapolis, MN 55419.

Contents

A Big Hit! 4

The Baseball Diamond.................. 22

Glossary 23

Index 24

Read More 24

Learn More Online...................... 24

About the Author 24

A Big Hit!

Crack!

My friend hits the ball with his bat.

Look at the ball fly!

It is time to play baseball.

Tomorrow is game day.

My friend is ready!

He learned to throw and catch with his team.

His **coach** showed them how to use a bat.

The night before a game, my friend is hungry.

He eats chicken and rice for dinner.

Healthy food gives his body **energy**.

9

Then, it is time for bed.

My friend goes to sleep early.

He needs lots of rest before a game.

When he wakes up, he puts on his **jersey**.

My friend's team dresses the same for the game.

He ties his **cleats**.

They help him run fast.

At the field it is sunny.

My friend puts on a hat.

This keeps the sun out of his eyes.

The team **stretches** to get loose.

They touch their toes.

Then, they warm up.

They throw and catch the ball.

The game starts.

My friend sits out first.

He cheers for everyone on the field.

Now, it is his turn to play.

My friend steps up to **home plate**.

I love baseball!

The Baseball Diamond

Baseball games are played on a field called a baseball diamond.

Players take turns hitting the ball. This is called being at bat.

If they hit the ball, they run around the diamond. Getting back to home plate gives the team a point.

Glossary

cleats shoes with bumps on the bottom for gripping the ground

coach the person who teaches and leads a sports team

energy the power to be active and do things

home plate the spot on a baseball field where people stand to bat

jersey a shirt worn by a player on a sports team

stretches moves in ways that pull muscles longer

Index

bat 4, 6, 22
coach 6
eat 8
game 6, 8, 10, 12, 18, 22
stretches 16
team 6, 12, 16, 22

Read More

Leed, Percy. *Baseball: A First Look (Read about Sports)*. Minneapolis: Lerner Publications, 2023.

Troupe, Thomas Kingsley. *Baseball (I Can Play Sports!)*. Minneapolis: Kaleidoscope, 2022.

Learn More Online

1. Go to **www.factsurfer.com** or scan the QR code below.
2. Enter **"Baseball Game"** into the search box.
3. Click on the cover of this book to see a list of websites.

About the Author

Emma Huddleston lives in St. Paul with her family. She enjoys playing sports and watching the Minnesota Twins play baseball!